Face to Face:
Encounters between Jews & Blacks

Photographs and text by
Laurence Salzmann

Trainer's Statement
Cheryl Cutrona

Preface by
Lenora Berson

Introduction by
Reverend Paul M. Washington, D.D., D.P.S.

A Blue Flower Book
Philadelphia, Pennsylvania

Special thanks to The Philadelphia Foundation and the
Alexis Rosenberg Foundation for helping to support the printing of 500 copies of this
edition of **Face to Face:** *Encounters between Jews & Blacks* for use by the Good
Shepherd Neighborhood House Mediation Program.

Printing by Becotte & Gershwin, Inc., U.S.A.
Designed by Barbara Torode

First Edition, 1996

Library of Congress Cataloging-in-Publication Data
Laurence Salzmann, 1944-
Face to Face: Encounters between Jews & Blacks by Laurence Salzmann, 1st edition.
ISBN 0-9603924-3-2:
1.United States Race relations. — 2. Jewish. — 3. African American. — 4. Anthropology.— 5. Oral history.

Trainer's Statement by Cheryl Cutrona
Preface by Lenora E. Berson
Introduction by Rev. Paul M. Washington
Photographs and text by Laurence Salzmann
Book design by Barbara Torode
A Blue Flower Book

Library of Congress Card Number: 95-80341

Face to Face

Encounters between Jews & Blacks

As mediators, the Mediation Program trainers are experienced third-party neutrals. We teach others to confront conflict constructively, be better listeners, and express anger without blame. We also realize that despite the protestations to the contrary, we all harbor biases based on personal experiences that have influenced how we view life, what we favor or disfavor about various people, how we behave and what we value. Biases stimulate conflict that can easily escalate and turn ugly. Unlearning stereotypes and being open to viewing each person as a unique individual is not a simple process. As facilitators of discussions on bias, racism and sexism, our job is to create a setting where workshop participants feel comfortable enough to develop a better understanding of each other, appreciate our differences, and celebrate common ground.

The Mediation Program staff hopes that by facilitating "Face to Face" workshops in neighborhoods throughout Philadelphia, we can foster understanding and improve ethnic relations.

If your group would like to host a "Face to Face" workshop in your community, call the Mediation Program at (215) 843-5413.

Cheryl Cutrona, Executive Director
Good Shepherd Neighborhood House Mediation Program

Introduction

One of my favorite authors is the late C. S. Lewis.

He was not a man schooled in theology. He was a professor of Medieval and Renaissance literature at Magdalene College in Cambridge, England, but he is best known for his writings on theological subjects.

In one of his many books I recall his having written:"Despite the many labels that differentiate us as races, classes, nationalities, colors, religions and languages, when human beings begin to relate to each other as human beings, we find that we all share far more similarities than dissimilarities."

Having been born in this country in the Twentieth Century, I found it incredible to read in Lerone Bennett's *Before the Mayflower* that before the year 1664, Whites did not even know that they were White. Most White colonists were indentured, subject to the same indignities as Black servants and slaves and held in the same contempt and that there was a strong bond of empathy between Blacks and Whites. Racism was a creature of political and economic imperatives. The observation of C. S. Lewis was and is fundamentally true. Human beings are far more similar to each other than dissimilar.

Some years ago I had the privilege to participate for an evening with the people who were involved in the Good Shepherd Neighborhood House Mediation Program. I was in the midst of the people who gave life, substance and meaning to this program. To look at them they had all of the labels mentioned above, but I soon found that those labels were superficial, and beneath them and beyond them I saw the commonality of our humanity. I saw people laboring to regain that one-ness of which we were robbed. I heard children and adults speaking about their mission to be mediators, to be the bridges reestablishing wholeness where brokenness seems to be the norm, reconciling where repudiation and rejection are so characteristic of our culture.

Did God really make us "Jew and gentile; bound and free," races which vie for superiority over other of God's children, all of whom are sacred, whom he made living souls? On this one island home, planet earth, is there such a thing as "outsiders and insiders," and in this life where we are all interdependent, can not the heart of a Black man give life to a White man, who can live without the other; can man live with-out woman, can the haves have were there not the have-nots, and in this land were not the Africans brought here as the very foundation of an economy?

Today it is so easy to despair. There is a lot of darkness covering our earth, but even with the grossness of the darkness, darkness does not prevail because it is punctured and punctuated by light. I have seen that light, people who light the candle rather than curse the darkness. For me the contents of this book is the living evidence of that light, and further-more we find our commonalty outweighing our differences, and that there is indeed goodness even when there seems to be so much that is bad.

To study the portraits presented to us by Laurence Salzmann in this book and listen to the words spoken by those portrayed, we will expe-rience "Face to Face" and we will be "a step closer" to that peace and har-mony for which our souls pray and long.

Rev. Paul M. Washington, D.D., D.P.S.
Rector Emeritus, The Church of the Advocate

Preface

In 1965 I was commissioned by the American Jewish Committee to study the 1964 Black riot in North Philadelphia. Thirty years ago the business infrastructure of North Philadelphia, which suffered severe damage in the riot, was still largely Jewish owned, a holdover from the twenties, thirties and forties when this area of the city had a large Jewish population.

In particular the American Jewish Committee wanted to know if the riot had been motivated, even in part, by anti-Semitism. I found no evidence that anti-Semitism was a motivating factor. However, in the course of my research, I uncovered a complex set of beliefs that Blacks held about Jews. In interviews for my book, *The Negroes and the Jews*, published in 1971, I found an equally confounding, complex and contradictory set of ideas held by Jews about Blacks.

In the mid sixties the public position of Blacks and Jews about each other was simple. They had common enemies and were therefore allies. As they say in politics, "the enemy of my enemy is my friend."

No other inter-group relationship has had so profound and so positive an effect on our political life, as the United States struggles to become the modern world's first inter-racial, multi-ethnic democratic society.

However, over the last three decades, much has happened to fray the political bonds that held Blacks and Jews together.

Jews have been fully integrated as individuals into American society while Blacks have found it necessary to use their number and their race as levers to pry open the doors of opportunity.

Close up, Blacks and Jews are as often antagonists as they are friends now, yet both regret the passing of an era of better feeling and worry about the larger consequences of their disunion to themselves and to the nation.

Documentary photographer Laurence Salzmann has correctly identified the crucial nature of the Black-Jewish relationship and has sought through the eye of his camera and the transcription of his subject's words to put a human face to the crisis in this emblematic alliance.

It is hard to overstate the importance of an emotional as well as an intellectual understanding of these intergroup dynamics, if we are, as a nation, to fulfill our promise as "the last best hope of the world."

Few works do this important job so well as *Face to Face: Encounters between Jews & Blacks*.

Lenora E. Berson

Introduction

Readers of scriptures in both churches and synagogues are familiar with the injunctions of Leviticus, that we should love our neighbors as ourselves and accord the same treatment to "the stranger that dwells with us." We have only to look at history, and to look around us, to see how difficult the human race finds it to practice that philosophy.

Laurence Salzmann's *Face to Face: Encounters between Jews & Blacks* juxtaposes through photographs and quotations how African Americans and Jews view each other, and by so doing reveals much about humor, human interaction, and coexistence in America. Throughout our history, Jews and African Americans have often felt a deep kinship. In the days of slavery, African Americans equated their plight with that of the Israelites in Egyptian bondage, and longed for their own Moses and Promised Land.

After emancipation, Jews who struggled against vicious prejudice and discrimination empathized with African Americans and built alliances with them to overcome the barriers both groups faced. In the twentieth century, African Americans and Jews have worked closely together around important social and political issues from trade unions to civil and political rights. Jews helped found the National Association for the Advancement of Colored People in 1909, and gave their lives during the voting drives in the South during the turbulent 1960s.

Over the last few decades, however, relations between African Americans and Jews have deteriorated over such controversies as Middle East peace and affirmative action. In many older American cities, relations between African Americans and Jews have become tense and confrontational. Somewhere, somehow, much of the old kinship and empathy has broken down. Indifference and open hostility have arisen, and perhaps more frighteningly, there has been a resurgence of the old name-calling and the old racial and religious slurs.

Understanding comes from dialogue and communication. Hate and fear arise from separation and ignorance. Laurence Salzmann's *Face to Face* is a good starting point for a thoughtful and constructive dialogue between African Americans and Jews, and between all Americans about the the subject of race and pluralism in American life. By studying his photographs and quotations, we learn that African Americans and Jews can share important values and commitments while recognizing their cultural differences. We may have miles to go to understand each other, but each step can be a blessing.

William H. Gray III

© Mordechai Rosennstein

God spoke to Moses Face to Face as a human being
would speak to his friend.

Exodus 33, 11

photograph circa 1951, by Reuben Goldberg

Nora, as we were accustomed to call her, was a part of all family activities. At a birthday party for my brother, Jacob, she stood next to him. She had baked a wonderful coconut cake. We thought of her as a member of the family. She always had sensible advice and, in effect, ran the house. In later years, she came to have her own spot at the dinner table with my mother and father. Nora, with little formal education, was wise beyond all belief. I am sorry that in her life I didn't try to learn more about her life and upbringing. Our lives pass before us too quickly and before we know it, it is time to go.

Artist's Statement

I was raised by a Black woman named Zenora Carter. She was from Virginia. She worked first as a maid to my grandmother and when my mother got married, came along, as part of my mother's dowry, so to speak. Zenora worked for our family her whole life. I dedicate this book to Zenora's Carter memory. She is certainly a big part of mine.

I used photo-text to explore and come to grips with my own racism, which I found to be increasing day by day. I found myself connecting my own personal experiences with crime to the negative images of Black men perpetuated every day by the media. I wanted to find out if Blacks were really as anti-Semitic as a recent study by the Anti-Defamation League suggests. It seems that Blacks and Jews still subscribe to stereotypes and misperceptions, ignoring the real dilemmas of their relationship. I set out on a journey of exploration, not to foreign lands, but to people living in diverse corners of Philadelphia with whom I had never had an opportunity to speak, to find answers to my questions.

My concerns about the Black-Jewish dialogue really grew out of my concerns about Black and White relations. At age 50, I found myself living in a part of the city that is almost 75 percent Black, yet not knowing a single Black person except for our mailman.

I couldn't say, "some of my best friends are Black," because the reality for me and most White people that I know was that that none of us had any Black friends. I wanted to understand why this was so; why our worlds are so separate.

I began to question the divided and divisive nature of American society where Blacks and Whites live in two very different worlds with shared borders. This entrenched practice of separation and exclusion helps to create the many problems confronting our society today.

As an American Jew, I chose at first to focus on the Jewish part of this troubling racial equation. I wanted to understand what it was that went wrong in the Jewish–Black relationship as a way of understanding this issue for the rest of society. I chose a photo-text format to explore answers to this dilemma.

Many of the Black people who spoke to me for this project were open in their assessments of the situation. Most Jews, while willing to talk privately about their feelings on the subject, were less willing to acknowledge publicly their true feelings.

The strength of the present work lies in its finely-tuned combination of imagery and words. The photo-text format provides a bridge between language and imagery, ie. the "cultural language" spoken by African Americans and Jews. It is filtered through the images, by means of facial expressions, posture, gestures. Thus words evoke images to reinforce their respective "realities." I feel that by generating a dialogue in which the players are helping to decode the myths we have of them, we might be able to find some resolution to the issues that separate us as a society.

The quotes presented here were selected from recorded interviews that I did with close to fifty people. I distilled their overall statements to present what I think is the essence of what they said. A study-guide which accompanies this book (available on the World Wide Web*) has been created to broaden the discussion raised by their quotes.

Although a few of the quotations may be considered provocative or controversial, visitors to the highly acclaimed "Face to Face" exhibit* found them the basis for a constructive dialogue among all Americans about race and pluralism in American life.

I felt that by sharing different viewpoints a dialogue could be engendered which might set the stage for a renewed understanding. If there is a bridge to be built, the stones are there.

Laurence Salzmann

* http://www.libertynet.org/~flower/
** First shown in Philadelphia under the title of Face to Face in collaboration with the work of photographer Don Camp at the National Museum of American Jewish History, Philadelphia in conjunction with Afro-American Historical & Cultural Museum's exhibit of Bridges and Boundaries. Show's title suggested by Richard Watson.

The Interviews

Willie "Junior" Baker came to Philadelphia from Wilmington, North Carolina in 1949. His first job was with the Shupak Pickle Company. Today, in his own pickle business, near Broad and Lehigh, he is assisted by his wife, son and daughter.

Willie Baker: Morris Shupak taught me some things about pickles. Pickles are basically made with garlic, salt water and vinegar. Everything is fresh fermentation. It is strictly a Jewish pickle.

Most Jewish people, they like them half green, and most Black people like them well done; that's pickles.

I wouldn't say that Jews and Blacks don't get along, 'cause like I say, I have very good friends who are Jewish. A man is only as good as his word.

If I was White, I would be much further in life, being Black has a lot to do with it. God has blessed me and brought me from a long way. An' so far, I am pretty happy. At least, I keep bread on the table.

Willie added that most older people ate more pickles than the younger generation, and that New York pickles are different from Philadelphia pickles; in New York, they don't use vinegar. His pickles put up in June and July are ready by the first of the year. The pickles come with Kosher certification.

Esther Burday, who keeps a Kosher home, is surrounded all day by pork products she herself would never eat. Her Red Joe's on Ridge Avenue is one Jewish-owned meat shop that still serves the Black community of North Philadelphia.

Esther Burday: This is the only business that our family ever knew. There were good times and there were bad times. As a child I didn't know that I had a father because he was here putting in 60 to 70 hours a week…. It is a seven-day-a-week operation.

In the winter season hog maws and chitlins are our biggest specialty. We are known for Virginia country hams. In the summertime it is ribs.

My customers are so poor that at the end of the month it breaks my heart that they come in and buy neck bones to make soup. They buy beans and they are making big pots of some kind of stew or something because there is no money to eat…. It hurts me.

Red Joe's had not been touched during the riots of 1965. Esther attributed that to the fact that the surrounding community respected and loved her late father. Esther, who took over the running of the store from her late husband, learned after she came to the store that her husband had indulged in eating all the pork products that she herself would not allow at home, including pigs' feet.

Anwar Husam Azim El: I had a teacher, Miss Sussman. She was a good teacher. A lot of Jewish teachers were concerned with the development and welfare of African-American children. They were sincere teachers but….

The but is that in business in the sixties and the fifties you had "so called" Jewish store owners and merchants who were exploiting the Black people.

Folks in America always want to develop dialogues with other people, but how are you going to learn to love somebody else when you hate yourself? Black folks in America got to learn to love each other.

One thing I know about Jewish people is that, if they are your friends, they are down with you to the end.

Anwar said that the Jewish merchants that he worked for would use unscrupulous business practices to take advantage of unsuspecting Black customers. He said that the customers were not only over-charged for products that they could have gotten cheaper elsewhere, but were often sold services that they didn't need at all.

Lou Malman and Alex Malman: It is very strained, very strained! You have to remember that a lot of Blacks have converted to the Muslim religion. A good percent. Blacks are not going to live with Jews or vice-versa, you understand? When you go by housing patterns in this city, it is very segregated. More segregated since the Civil War. This city was more integrated in the thirties and forties. You have to remember that this was a Jim Crow city. They didn't sit in the back on the trolley, but it was Jim Crow all the way. Jews made money here because it was a ghetto, not because the Blacks were being exploited, but because they couldn't go anywhere else. The civil rights laws destroyed North Philadelphia, not the riots.

*T*heir statement concerning the Civil Rights laws infers that when Blacks were free to shop downtown, they took their business there. This resulted in a loss of business to the local merchants, many of whom were Jewish. Till then, Blacks were not made welcome in Philadelphia's downtown department stores. The Malman Brothers are like a living history book, recalling events that many of us no longer remember or never knew about.

Zachary Marcus Cesare Harris' interpretation of history provides him a view of the Black-Jewish dynamic that is not all that unusual in some parts of the Black community, yet one that is troubling and the cause of much consternation to those in the Jewish community.

Zachary Marcus Cesare Harris:

There is gonna be a degree of separation and integration on both sides.

More or less it is up to Blacks to be more wary of things that are going down and to support organizations that are positive to them. If a Black comes off about what Jews do and say something he is called anti-Semitic.

How can a Black be called anti-Semitic when we are the true Semites? But yet when the JDL* goes off and does something they are not called anti-Black or anti-White. Blacks can't be racist because we are not in power. To be racist you must be in the ruling class and must have the power to execute discriminatory acts towards others based on their race, creed or color.... We are not the ruling class.

*Jewish Defense League.

Zachary continued, "Jews identify with Israel, yet Israel has identified itself with the enemies of Blacks. No matter how much, quote, unquote, the Jews and Blacks get along in America, it is just the icing on the cake. The reality is you are showing one thing, but on a deeper level, something else. Basically we are just like the Tuskegee experiment: inject twenty-two Black males with syphilis, but tell them that you are doing some good Same thing with the AIDS scare in Africa...."

David Auspitz: is the owner of a well known deli-restaurant. Often he tells it like he sees it. His staff is all Black and David says that one day it is not inconceivable that the his place will be Black-owned as well. He believes hard work to be the answer.

David Auspitz: I think as you have the upward mobility in the Black community that they have adapted or, at least, publicly expounded what might have been hidden before – the same anti-Semitic viewpoints as the rest of the world.

Blacks are having a horrible time explaining the Koreans and the other Asian immigrants… how they walked into this country about seven seconds ago and have jumped into first place in education and business and everything else. Meanwhile, the Blacks are still wandering around talking about "I'm suppressed, I'm suppressed."

Instead of making the Jew a target for my own problems, I would reach out and make the Jew a stepping stone for my success. If you offer a Jew an inch, he will give you back six miles in help.

David Auspitz in his rhetoric does not take into account the many basic differences that separate the Jewish and Black communities. That one group came with all the hope of new immigrants, the other with the legacy of slavery, does not enter into his calculation

Lynne Abraham has gained a national reputation as District Attorney of Philadelphia, advocating the death penalty in homicide cases. In her political campaigns, the Black electorate has overwhelmingly supported her. Could she win running against a Black candidate?

Lynne Abraham: I think there was a feeling of brotherhood because both Blacks and Jews were an oppressed group. You could argue about who was more oppressed, but that doesn't get you anywhere.

There has been a lot of controversy over how much Jews and Blacks really had.

It is the terrible crime problems that rip at the heart of the relationship, which is made worse by sensational journalism. I call them the "vampire press." They are only interested in hysteria and the bloodier and the more divisive, the more newspapers it sells.

I think we have to understand that we all are on this little piece of earth for a short time. There is enough room at the table for everybody.

Lynne continued: "We have to be able to tell the extremist on either side (that includes the Meir Kahane types and Louis Farrakhan radical people) that we have heard your act before and it is bor-oh-ring, doesn't apply to us go peddle your hatred someplace else." Lynne is constantly on the move learning first hand about the concerns of the citizens of the city. Here she is with Minister David Weeks, Jr., of Shalom Baptist Church of Logan.

Robin's Book Store on South 13th Street in Philadelphia is often the venue for readings by Black authors and poets. Larry's love of Black literature led him to organize the annual celebration of Black writing in 1982. It is a much looked-forward-to event on the African-American cultural calender with people in attendance from everywhere.

Larry Robin: I have trouble with the issue of race and, I guess, religion. I am Jewish but I never thought of myself as being Jewish.

The Civil Rights Movement was a galvanizing force. When SNCC* decided to get rid of the Whites from the movement, people took it as a personal affront. Stokely Carmichael said, you know if I am talking about you, and if you are guilty…you are guilty and if you are not, then you are not.

The situation for the Black middle-class is better than it was; for Blacks as a race it is not. The statistics about young Black males are frightening. Charges of genocide are defensible. What else do you call it when 70 percent of your males end up dead or in jail?

*The Student Non-Violent Coordinating Committee

Larry's view is that most of the attitudes that are blamed on race are probably more class oriented than race oriented. He said, "Jim Crow was really a class econom creation to keep the populist movement from succeeding and it succeeded wonderfully well!"

Lamont stated that he is a searcher for truth and justice. He once worked for a local TV station as news editor but quit because he felt the news they presented distorted the truth. His latest book of poetry, Dusty Road, a Vietnam Suite, is about his experiences in Vietnam.

Lamont B. Steptoe: My mother, God rest her soul, worked for a prominent Pittsburgh Jewish family for twenty years. They lived in a very exclusive area of Pittsburgh called Squirrel Hill, which is predominantly Jewish.

My brother-in-law discovered that her employer was not paying Social Security for her and they had to be legally made to do so. We were very, very poor.

Mother would bring home *gefilte* fish and *matzo* balls and we would eat Jewish foods. Talk among the domestics was, it was understood, that this was one way as a group of people they, rather than give you physical dollars, would give you food and used clothing. On one level it could be understood as an act of philanthropy; on another, a kind of very clever manipulation.

Lamont is much inspired by Walt Whitman whom he considers to be a "mediummistic poet"— a poet inspired by the muses. That is why it was only appropriate that he be photographed standing in front of a wall on which was written Whitman's words, "I am large, I contain multitudes." The mural, based on a painting by Sydney Goodman, was painted by the Anti-Graffiti Network.

Mordechai Rosenstein, a noted Hebrew calligrapher and artist, didn't want to comment about Jews and Blacks. He said that that was a question for people who dealt with issues of race relations. He was willing though, to share his memories of Jewish life in Strawberry Mansion as he knew it.

Mordechai Rosenstein: We moved about 1939 or 1940 to Strawberry Mansion. It was a residential inner-city neighborhood: narrow streets, stores on every corner. Jewish was in the air. It was really like a ghetto, although not every family on the street was Jewish.

Strawberry Mansion had been a German neighborhood. We moved out in 1948. It wasn't so much a flight but in 1949, 1950, the Northeast was the ultimate. A guy could buy a house with a driveway, with a garage to park your car, with a playground, with the new school. You could live, you could see the sky. You stand on Douglas Street you see how narrow the sky looks. Clouds could be coming, you didn't see them 'til they were overhead, you didn't know if it was going to rain.

On Douglas Street, Mordechai met Jolanda Cooke and daughter, Beatrice. They now live in the house that Mordechai's family once occupied. Mordechai's old synagogue, Etz Chaim ve Zichron Jacob, is now the Faith Temple Church of God in Christ.

Patsy has worked for Marilyn for 22 years as a monogrammer. Together they find ways to laugh at life's difficulties. Milton Street in East Mt. Airy, where Patsy lives, was all Jewish when she moved there in 1969 but soon became all Black.

Patricia J. Jones: Marilyn is my ace. She is not like a boss, she is like a sister. When I was sick she took care of me. I call her my honky sister and she calls me her soul sister.

Marilyn Wolf: I liked Patsy first as a person before I began to see her virtues as a worker. She has a great sense of humor. Many times over the years her kids have worked here. Now her grand-children work here. She has a wonderful family.

I find that the people out here were very prejudiced both against Blacks and Jews. When we moved in here 14 years ago this guy came out with a big German shepherd and said, "this dog is here to keep out Jews and niggers." I mean blatant out he told us. He said that's why the neighborhood goes down, Jews and niggers.

While hate mongers might heap equal insults on both Patricia and Marilyn, in their own relationship they remain unequals. Perhaps that is inevitable in an employer-employee relationship. Many feel that the rift in the Jewish-Black relationship is nourished by the great economic divide that separates the two groups.

Isidore Hofferman's work as a jobber selling cloth takes him to all parts of the city, but his real loves are people and social justice. His concern for making the world a better place led him to join the board of the Mary Rouse Child Care Center.

Isidore Hofferman: Twenty years ago, we in the Shalom Aleichem Club wanted to have contact with Black groups so that we could meet on a mutual basis and find out about each other. It is a funny thing, we have gotten so close that we don't even think about the Jewishness and the Blackness, which is the way it should be…. If you know people you forget about the stereotypes.

When ethnic rivalries get in the way we don't look at each other as people. In Yugoslavia, people lived peacefully for years, and the Croats, the Bosnians and the Serbs would still continue to do that if it were not for these so-called leaders that are out for themselves. If you don't know someone, you can believe anything that someone else would want to propagandize.

Nellie Parker is a community activist who is on the board of the Mary Rouse Child Care Center at 3rd and Dauphin Streets. In addition to a full-time job as a mental health worker, Nellie also has time to look after her 23 grandchildren.

Nellie Parker: Izzy is the closest Jewish friend that I have and that is because we go back so far. We go back 25 years.

I treat Izzy not as a Jewish guy but as a human being. If we have words, it is not because he is a Jew. It is because it was something that we had to get off our chests. If we are ever to get together we have to look beyond race.

There is bad and good in every race. I shouldn't hold against you what someone else of your race did. A lot of people will stigmatize you because you are Black. Just being Black automatically makes you like everybody else and that is wrong. Give me a chance. I am who I am, you know, I might be the best person in the world and never did anything to anybody. Why would you prejudge me to be a bad person?

26-27 *When Izzy and Nellie posed for this photograph, a car with a lone Black man drove up. It was uncertain as to what the driver might want. He turned out to be Nellie's husband. As he didn't recognize that it was Izzy who had his arm around his wife he was a little taken aback. Nellie said, "It's just Izzy, go on home!"*

Leon Bass: The big problem confronting us today is how do we, as human beings, relate to one another. Maybe some incidents or events will happen to us where we want to place the blame on people because of racial and religious differences. We tend to blame everybody for the acts of maybe one or two. We have to be able to rise above that and try to look at people as human beings. It is a very difficult thing to do.

I saw what people can do when they say you are not good enough. You are not worthy because you're Jewish, or you're Polish, or you're handicapped, or you're a gypsy and I knew that if I had been in Germany at the time I, too, would have been put in that concentration camp, because I was told that I wasn't good enough, back in my own country.

Leon was upset about the withdrawing from further showing of The Liberators, *a film about Black soldiers who had participated in liberating some concentration camps. The film's critics claimed that they were not liberators. Leon said it's simply racism raising its ugly head once again. Whenever anyone wants to say something positive about Blacks, there is someone there to deny it.*

Kofi Asante is a man who brings to his convictions great elan and energy. He is a musician, producer and teacher. What is most outstanding about him is his commitment to teaching young people about their heritage through music. Lenora said he is always fun to be with.

Kofi Asante: In my household we were raised not to hate, not to look at the color of a person's skin, but to look at who you are inside. I was raised by three Black women: my mother, my grandmother, and my great-grandmother. Their whole thing was when you go out in the world you have to be the best that you can be for who you are, and

(continued on page 32)

Lenora E. Berson is author of The Negroes and The Jews. As Director of special projects in Mayor Goode's Administration, she helped Kofi Asante produce his first Aframericas Festival. The Kente cloth worn by Lenora was a gift to her from Kofi.

Lenora E. Berson: The sentimental notions that Jews had about Blacks and that Blacks had about Jews have exploded. It is important to understand where the mythology started and also to see what the history really was. Jews viewed Blacks as people that were somehow like Jews in the old country who, given the opportunities Jews were

(continued on page 33)

Kofi referred to his dear friend Leonora as a kind of soldier who having researched and wrote about the differences and similarities of African Americans and Jews had had to struggle to make her views known. He said, "she is the queen of the riverboat gamblers."

Kofi Asante*

nobody is greater than you, and you are not greater than anybody else.

I had at least two or three very strong spiritual revelations where certain things happened that made me think about what I was really doing, that pushed me towards looking at music as my salvation. One of the real turning points for me was when I found out that I was of it and not it, and that I am a real small micro dot in a very large situation.

The gut of who I am says that God is at the end of every door and that as much as we see those things that separate us, there are a lot of things that can keep us together....

*Kofi Asante's name was given to him in a religious ceremony by an African Priestess. Asante was an African king in 14 BCE. The name Kofi comes from the West African language Twi, and means "the good man."

Lenora E. Berson

given, would become like Jews. Jews were seen by Blacks as Biblical people with a similar history. Hadn't they been slaves in Egypt? Jews were part of the promised land but they turned out to be White Americans.

But Jews, unlike most other White groups, value the good opinion of Blacks and desire a partnership with them.

There still is a political and ideological relationship because politically, Blacks and Jews are still largely in the liberal camp. In Congress—a very interesting thing, to date—the Black caucus has never voted against Israel.

What's important is that Blacks and Jews remain political allies. If Jews can accept that they have "Arafatized" Farrakhan, and Blacks can respect Jewish concerns about quotas, our relationship can be maintained.

In 1989, Larry Pitt and Lana Felton-Ghee organized the Philadelphia-to-Philadelphia project, which took 2000 Philadelphia school children to Philadelphia, Mississippi, to commemorate the deaths of Civil Rights workers Chaney, Goodman and Schwerner.

Larry Pitt: Two areas that are divisive to Blacks and Jews are quotas and Louis Farrakhan…. As far as quotas, there is a difference between quotas that are meant to exclude and quotas that are meant to include…. You don't have to dismiss a person one hundred percent as a result of one or two things that he said. I heard Minister Farrakhan

(continued on page 36)

Lana Felton-Ghee said her trip to Mississippi provided the opportunity to thank personally the mothers of James Chaney, Michael Goodman and Andrew Schwerner for the sacrifice their sons had made to insure the civil rights of us all today.

Lana Felton-Ghee: Certain things you just cannot discuss. What we have to do is come together to the point of respect. A Black person's point of view on the quota system is based on our history. It's not likely that we are going to concede that to anybody. That is one issue that the Jewish

(continued on page 37)

Since their trip down south and before Larry an[d] Lana have remained friends. They have both a busi[ness] and personal relationship. As a lawyer, Lar[ry] processes compensation claims of workers for on-the job injuries. Lana has worked in the health, union an[d] political fields.

Larry Pitt

speak when I was in Africa at the African-American sum-mit. He gave an electrifying speech. What he was talking about was engendering what amounts to a feeling of Zionism among African Americans for Africa.

It is very hard to get yourself out of your own mind set and to see the situation from the viewpoint of somebody else. Not many people can do that. That is the first step in trying to understand why.

There are far more areas of mutual interest politically than of dissension. The majority of Blacks and Jews tend to look at things from a similar vantage point, somewhat cen-ter-to-left of the political spectrum.

The historic tie that developed during the civil rights movement was based on a similar outlook on human rights and the overall connection that stems from historic experi-ences as oppressed minorities.

Lana Felton-Ghee

community has a point of view on. And quite frankly, I don't see either of us coming together and saying, "OK, I agree with your point of view." The same as it relates to Reverend Jesse Jackson and Minister Louis Farrakhan....

We have to look at individual situations. There are certain things I don't discuss with Larry because I believe that it is disrespectful for me to discuss these things with him.

He must maintain a loyalty to the Jewish community and he respects the fact that I must maintain a loyalty to the African American community. We are not talking about criminal acts, we are talking about political points of view.

Eleanor W. Myers is a graduate of the University of Pennsylvania Law School. For three years Myers directed Woman's Way. She has taught business ethics. Presently, she is an associate professor at Temple University School of Law. Her husband is a lawyer.

Eleanor W. Myers: I identify myself first as a woman and secondarily as a Jew and thirdly as a mother and fourth as a lawyer, and down the list somewhere as a wife.

Recently, a Black Bar Association officer spoke about the relatively few Black men in law school. To make his point, he complained **that there were more Black women than Black men in law school.** This comparison upset me because I thought he could have made his point by other comparisons which did less damage, as I saw it, to the place and accomplishments of Black women. I asked Muriel what she thought about his comment and she said she didn't hear it, or at least did not hear it the way I did. She and I hear things differently based on our experiences. It is exploring those differences together that is so interesting and so troubling. It is troubling because there is a part of her, a big part, that I can't truly appreciate.

Muriel Morisey Spence attended Radcliffe as an undergraduate and holds a law degree from Georgetown University Law Center. She worked for 20 years in the U.S. Congress and was an aide to Shirley Chisholm. Presently she is an assistant professor at Temple University School of Law.

Muriel Morisey Spence: If I had to say what is going to be the trigger or the decision base that drives me most it is going to be racial. It is very hard to grow up in a racist society and not live out the behavior that comes with it, which is separation. What racism does, it separates people and they live separate lives.… **It is not a problem, Black women in law school, but that opportunity is limited for Black men….**

The amazing thing to me is that any White person is prepared to make friends with a Black person. I mean, if I were White I don't know how many Black friends I would have because the whole society would be telling me, "they are not equal, they are not worthy; you must be in some rebellious state to reach out to a Black person." I think that is what society tells White people.

40-41: *Eleanor's son, Jesse, and Muriel's son, Andrew, are classmates at a Quaker school. The question is: When they grow up will they be able to cross the racial and cultural divides that leave their mothers not always understanding things in the same way?*

In 1975 Miriam Mednick became the founding director of the Comprehensive Services for School Age Parents Program that provides parenting education and child care services for teenage mothers. Miriam, although retired, continues to be active in civic affairs.

Miriam Mednick: Marilyn and I worked together professionally and we also became friends. We shared an approach of how we wanted to administer this particular program. We have never had any tension between us. We have always agreed as to what the approach should be.

I have always felt that the problem is not one of color

(continued on page 44)

For many years, Marilyn Rivers and Miriam Mednick worked together in the Comprehensive Services for School Age Parents Program. Marilyn, who headed that program for nine years, is now the executive director of the Women's Christian Alliance.

Marilyn Rivers: When I met Miriam we immediately felt a bond. I felt good about her. She became a mentor and a friend. Our country is basically a racist society. Whenever the problems that affect the whole become overwhelming, we target those that we are used to blaming for the situation. There are all kinds of ways to make the problems the

(continued on page 45)

Mariyln and Miriam relate to each other as equals. Maryiln is pleased to aknowledge Miriam's role as mentor. The two women find that they agree on many diverse issues.

Miriam Mednick

but one of poverty. You see it as Black because a greater percentage of Black people are poor, so that the numbers come out in a big city like Philadelphia as more Black, because on a percentage basis there are more Blacks who are poor than Whites.

Miriam on the subject of Black teen pregnancy:

There is much more support among Black families for a teenager to have the baby than there is among White families now. That is a cultural difference. Another element is that because Black mothers have very high standards for their daughters, their daughters are much less likely to tell their mothers that they are pregnant until it is too late to have an abortion. A White teenager will more likely tell her mother within the first trimester than a Black girl because a Black teenager knows how much she is disappointing her mother. Would you agree?

Marilyn Rivers

problem of African Americans in this country and not recognize that they are happening to the whole. That is what happens in a racist society. The people that you are used to blaming for the problems are the people that you heap more blame on when the problems get bad for everybody.

Marilyn on the subject of White teen pregnancy:

One of the problems in the illegitimacy rate is the fact that more White girls have abortions. They have abortions because they are financially able to do so. It is much more of a stigma for them to have a baby out of wedlock. So, the issue around the rate of pregnancy is different from that of the rate of birth. The data shows that there is an increase in the number of White girls that get pregnant as adolescents and a decrease among the Black girls, but then the birth rate shows something different, because it doesn't look at the abortion issue.

Kimberly Creamer (center) and Katrina Scruggs (left) are two of the many children that George Weiss, through his Say Yes program, has guaranteed a college education. Say Yes is more than a scholarship, it is a challenge for us all.

George Weiss: I said to myself that if God ever gave me the financial wherewithal to make a difference in this life I would do it in the form of education. I was not singling out Black or White kids, I was just trying to make a difference.

In the inner city there is a condition of no hope. What you learn about the Say Yes kids is that they are as bright as any kids but they don't have the same advantages. These kids have the deck stacked against them.

The expectations that I have for the Say Yes kids are the same that I have for my two natural daughters. What I want them to do is not turn their back on the inner city but to help other people make a difference, because that is how you break the chain.

George Weiss is among the many Jewish philanthropist who have given generously to Black education. Among the more well known there is Julius Rosenwald who a early as 1911 wrote, "I appeal to all high-minded men and women to join in a relentless crusade against race prejudice, indulgence in which will result in the blotting out of the highest ideals of our proud nation."

Eden Jacobowitz was a nineteen-year-old University of Pennsylvania undergraduate in 1993. His "water buffalo" epithet gained him notoriety and national recognition. The "water buffalo" case became a cause celebre for advocates of free speech.

Eden Jacobowitz: The main misunderstanding is what I said. "Water buffalo" by itself is not racial, but in the context of all these other epithets, it surely is, but I didn't know that real racial statements were shouted earlier.

The Hebrew word for water buffalo is *behemah*, which means a silly beast. It doesn't mean anything derogatory or particular to any race. It is usually used between Jews. You know, if someone is doing something that is odd or interrupting a class, the Rabbi would say "stop it you are acting like a *behemah*!" What this case really is, it is just a case of somebody saying "Shut up!" out the window. "Shut up you water buffalo!" and it turning into a racial case because of the total breakdown of communication.

Much was written about the "water buffalo" case. It was a CNN news item and a thorn in the side of Sheldon Hackney, then the president of the University of Pennsylvania. The case divided the campus into two very separate camps, each side thinking that its own position was correct.

Nikki Taylor, was a student at Penn in January of 1993 when she along with 18 of her Delta Sigma Theta sorority sisters had racial epithets yelled at them. The resulting "water buffalo" case with its implicit racist and sexist statements has never been correctly understood.

Nikki Taylor: …[H]is explanations don't sit right with me…. He claims he heard other people shouting slurs. If he heard someone else yelling, "*nigger*," why would he think to join in? The words hurt because of the context in which, they were said… He called us "water buffalo." I heard "black water buffalo." …[I]t still is an animal. It is a beast of burden and that is the same notion which enslaved my people. The notion that we were animals likened to beasts and that we are not fit to be humans.

I said, "Eden, I can help you to understand what it is like for me." He said, "I know because of the Holocaust…." But there we have a different experience. Yours is over; mine continues. There is a legacy that slavery left and it is called racism.

Tensions between Black and White students still continue at most American universities. At Penn, they just happened to be played out between a Jewish and Black student. If those so privileged to attend our nation's top schools act in ways that show a lack of tolerance for each other, what hope is there for the rest of the populace?

In 1993, Daniel Schwartz and Sarita Taylor (center, p.54-55) participated in Operation Understanding. Daniel would like to go into policics later in life. This interest is perhaps encouraged by his mother, Pennsylvania State Senator Allyson Y. Schwartz.

Daniel Schwartz: I hope to better my understanding of Jewish culture and of Afro-American culture. I would like to, with other members of the group and on my own, work to better relations between these two groups. We have learned already through Operation Understanding* orientation programs that Blacks and Jews have worked together in the civil rights movement but have grown apart.

What we need to do is realize that there is a coalition that can be built, and that we need to rebuild it and work towards better racial harmony in the whole country, not just between Blacks and Jews.

*The program initiated by United Negro College Fund President William H. Gray III with the help of his friend, George M. Ross, a prominent Philadelphia Jewish businessmen, promotes better understanding between high-school-age Blacks and Jews.

Operation Understanding sends six Jewish and six Black students each year to Senegal and Israel. The program designed to foster an understanding that the students will share with others in their community when they return. The are expected to make a commitment to work for better racial understanding throughout life.

In 1993, Sarita Taylor was the president of Central High School's Student Association. She is very active in her church and her speech is full of enthusiam for things that she would like to accomplish in life. Sarita, now a college student, would like to become a television network anchorwoman.

Sarita Taylor: I have never really understood the Jewish community. I always used to think of them as the victims. I have only heard about the Holocaust. I never learned about their culture, their religion or them as people. Back in the sixties and the fifties a lot of signs that said "No Blacks" also followed with "No Jews" and "No dogs."

A lot of our Jewish and Afro American problems stem from the fact that we were once so close. It's almost like we have broken our ties with each other… If a family member were to do something to another family member, you take it more to heart. If we begin to rebuild where we left off and if we kind of recapture what we once had and try to work together to kind of put it back together, then we could end a lot of the things that have been going on.

54-55 *At Central High School, as at many schools, groups seem to voluntarily segregate themselves. The Blacks sit with Blacks, the Asians with the Asians, the Hispanics with the Hispanics, the Whites with the Whites. It is a kind of segregation that seems to be endemic to our society.*

Leslie and Steven Field hired Ethel Pugh to help care for their adopted son, Harry. In her, they found a nurturing grandmother figure who will help keep Harry in touch with his Black identity. One of the problems of cross-racial adoption is maintaining that identity.

Leslie Jane Field: We adopted Harry, our son, who is Black, when he was four days old. We adopted Harry because we wanted a second child and we didn't care what color the child was, just as long as the child was healthy.

You don't know what prejudice is until you feel it yourself. It's virtually impossible for someone who is White to feel the full thrust of prejudice unless something unusual happens to you which allows you to experience those feelings. In our case, Harry has happened to us. And when people see Harry and me together, nine times out of ten, they assume that my husband is Black and the looks that I get, they could kill. If you are White you just don't know what hate feels like, simply because of the color of your skin….

Strides have been made, people are more accepting, but it is more on a very superficial level.

Leslie said, "I don't think Jewish people think of themselves as prejudiced. Yet most were unaware of how degrading the word schvartser, *once used by many Jews to describe Blacks, was to Black people. Schvartser, which means 'black' in Yiddish, has other meanings as well.*

Rachel grew up in Mt.Airy, a middle class neighborhood of Philadelphia where Blacks and Whites live harmoniously together. She studied filmmaking and photography and teaches both on the college level. She hopes soon to get back to film and video production.

Rachel Allender: I was raised by parents who had issues about Judaism that they never really examined. They never had race as an issue, they had Judaism as an issue. At a base level, they just assumed that their children would partner with people who were Jewish. If I had met a man who was Black and Jewish, I think that they would have

(continued on page 60)

Rodney is an artist-muscian who has been able to find a way to make his music speak to the concerns he has for building a better community by working with inner-city kids to create programs which help to build positive identity.

Rodney Whittenberg: Growing up in my house there were a lot of different messages. My dad grew up very, very poor, but worked his butt off to become a middle-class African-American. In his quest to be more middle-class, he went through a lot of distortion to fit what was expected of him, giving up a lot of what was part of his culture.

(continued on page 61)

Rachel and Rodney who went out together for several years had thought about marrying. Their relationship ended not so much over issues of race but because, in a manner of speaking, they outgrew each other. They still remain good friends and speak with each other frequently.

Rachel Allender

been very comfortable with that. The Black men that I have gone out with have all been men who were raised in middle class White neighborhoods, not in Black communities.

My grandmother got very upset when she learned that I was going out with Rodney. She said that if we had children that we would bring enormous pain into our lives. She couldn't use racist arguments. She said that our children would really suffer, that we would be ostracized!

The big joke in the family is that Rod paved the way with my grandmother for my present partner, he isn't Jewish, but, thank God he is White!

What I find most disquieting about Judaism is that at its core, Judaism attempts to segregate and to keep its clan together through a kind of segregation that I am not willing to accept.

Rodney Whittenberg

There was definitely a way of thinking that White culture was better.

In the Black community there has always been the idea that White women are a prize. That it is something that shows you have arrived, that you are, like, better than the other Black males, that you fit in, that you are accepted, that you are in some ways validated.

One of the saddest things to me about Black-Jewish relations is the lack of education about each other on both sides. Black people don't see Jewish people as any different than any other White people. They don't understand how they have been ostracized….

The other side of it is that most of the Jews follow along the line of every other group that wants to succeed in America, which is to assimilate…to make yourself more White, to make yourself fit in to the ideal.

Carol Rosenbaum Caleb is a free-lance video writer/producer/director. She lives with her husband and daughter in what is considered to be a dangerous area of the city. Yet, her particular street in East Germantown is set off by beautiful gardens with sweet-smelling flowers.

Carol Rosenbaum Caleb: An attitude exists that Black people are less than Jewish people, that they are not as smart. I think that a lot of people believe that and that's a tragedy. If people allow themselves to know each other, these biases usually disappear.

(continued on page 64)

J. Rufus Caleb is associate professor of English at the Community College of Philadelphia and a playwright. He grew up in Coatesville where Blacks and Whites were not as segregated This, he said, led to his being comfortable around Whites.

J. Rufus Caleb: My family's perspective has always been, how is the other person treating one of ours? They saw immediately the kind of relationship that Carol and I had and accepted the relationship. The backdrop of that is that independent of our relationship both families are very tolerant. Simply tolerant people.

(continued on page 64)

Carol and Rufus were bemused by the ditty that their daughter Sarah recited: "Miss Lucy had a baby. She named him Tiny Tim. She put him in the bathtub, to see if he could swim. He drank up all the water; he ate up all the soap; he tried to eat the bathtub, but it wouldn't go down his throat." It was one of many clapping rhymes she had learned in the neighborhood.

Carol Rosenbaum Caleb:

After a long time of hiding the relationship with Rufus from my mother, which made me real uncomfortable, I came to her and said, "I am almost 40, do you want me to be alone the rest of my life?"

That was the question that absolutely turned her around. That was her epiphany. She just suddenly came to a realization and did a 360 degree turn. It was a total acceptance from that moment on of the situation and of Rufus, and she loves him as if he were born to her. It is a real genuine love.

J. Rufus Caleb:

The African American community has always been a tolerant community—not unique in that way—more typical than atypical.

I have concluded that someone who is intolerant of me is generally an intolerant person. I don't think that the bad person is a bad person in just one small area. If you are unable to accept others from a specific culture then it generally means that you have real limits. With both Carol's brother, mother and father, there is a level of tolerance that reminds me of the level of tolerance in my family.

Sarah Elizabeth Caleb (opposite page) is being raised in an environment where there are other children of mixed racial backgrounds. Her parents feel that the outside world will give her a Black identity no-matter-what; however, Carol would like Sarah to have some knowledge of the Jewish traditions that were part of her experience.

Gamaliel Respes lives together with his wife Joyce and two children, son, Avidon Mikael, and daughter, Yasminah Tikvah, in a surburban New Jersey community. A friend said, their color and religion set them apart from neighbors who see them not as being Jewish but as being Black.

Gamaliel Respes: Being Jewish is a positive and we have always looked at it that way. When individuals see us, especially *Ashkenazi* Jews, they would say, "you have two strikes against you, one, you are Black, two, you are Jewish."

I realize that there are different bloods. I don't believe there is any person in the world who can say that they are still pure.

Society places certain labels on individuals. For example, because of the color of my skin, some people call me a Black, relating my identity simply to the color of skin.

We as human beings from the time of Adam had to label or name something in order to know it. My identity is a Jewish identity, primary and foremost. Secondarily, I have to realistically deal with the social prejudices that would affect a person of color here in the United States.

The Respes' family who practiced Jewish traditions for many years were officially converted to Judaism in 1973. At Passover, each year during their family's Seder, they commemorate freedom from slavery first, i Egypt and then again in the United States.

Lani Guinier's nomination for a position in the Clinton Administration's office of civil rights was withdrawn after an unfriendly press labeled her the "quota queen." She is now working to create a national dialogue on race, an issue central to her life.

Lani Guinier: There was a marked contrast between going to visit my father's family, as opposed to going to visit my mother's family. When we went to visit my father's family there was a huge embrace. We were lovingly welcomed. When we went to visit my mother's family it was as if we were coming from another planet.

Jews have the option of being White and it is a privilege that Jews in America enjoy. They are much more comfortable thinking about themselves as similarly oppressed people without recognizing that very critical asymmetry in the American experience.

In my [White] mother's case what surprised her most was that her father, who was the son of a Rabbi and prided himself on being an intellectual, was the most opposed to her marriage [to a Black man].

Lani lives with her husband, Noland, and son, Nikola, in a home which has a yard large enough to have a good catch. Lani told a story of how as a child her mother had taken her to a Hanukkah party where the other children shunned her. From that time on, she said, her mother knew that she wasn't going to raise Lani as a Jew.

Marie Amey Taylor: Being able to combine my desire to make a difference and to have people experience their own humanity and connect with each other is what really motivates me.

I see in a certain way, the relationship between African Americans and American Jews as a microcosm of what race relations is, and can be, in this country because I see those two groups as having as many reasons to hate each other and fall out with each other as they do to embrace each other and walk together.

If these two groups can get together with their love-hate relationship, with all of their stereotypic notions about each other that they are embarrassed to hold, with all of their history, then I think there is hope for any two groups to get together.

Tyrone Sabir: If Blacks and Jews have the same problem as anybody else it is because of hate. People hate each other because of lack of understanding of who they are and what they are.

This is the world problem. There is no love given. You've got Moslems killing Moslems, you've got Christians killing Christians, you've got Jews killing Jews. It's all over the world. Why? Because one dislikes another for some trivial, tri-vi-al, reason. It has nothing to do with anything strong but the weakest part of anything they find to exploit.

We are all creatures of the same creator. We all breathe one air, drink one water, use one earth, one land, and have a common bond. The only thing that makes us different is our piety.

Rabbi Brian Walt: The reality is that American Jews are one of the richest ethnic groups in the richest country in the world and African-Americans are probably the poorest.

In the Philadelphia area most Jews live secure, even comfortable lives, while over 40 percent of African-American children in the city grow up in homes with incomes below the poverty datum line.

It is a profound switch for Jews to think of ourselves as privileged. Our civilization and its values, and above all our self perception is based on our historical experience as victims. Breaking through this isolation, and joining with African-Americans to rebuild the community we share, will help us as Jews to be true to our people's legacy and its values.

Additional reading

Berman, Paul, ed. *Blacks and Jews: Alliances and Arguments*. New York: Delacorte Press, 1994.

_____. "The Other and the Almost the Same," The New Yorker, Feb. 28, 1994 p 61.

Berson, Lenora E. *The Negroes and the Jews*. New York: Random House, 1971.

Branch, Taylor. *Parting the Waters: America in the King Years, 1954-1963*. New York: Simon and Schuster, 1988.

Carmichael, Stokely. *Black Power: The Politics of Liberation in America*. New York: Random House, 1967.

Carson, Clayborne. *In Struggle: SNCC and the Black Awakening of the 1960s*. Cambridge MA: Harvard University Press, 1981.

Carson, Clayborne. "The Politics of Relations Between African-Americans and Jews", in *Blacks and Jews: Alliances and Arguments*. Edited by Paul Berman. New York: Delcorte Press, 1994. pp. 131- 43

Cose, Ellis. *The Rage of a Privileged Class*. New York: HarperCollins, 1993.

Day, Beth. *Sexual Life Between Blacks and Whites: The Roots of Racism*. New York: World Publications, 1972.

Dinnerstein, Leonard. "Anti-Semitism in America," in *African -American Attitudes, 1930's- 1990's*. New York: Oxford University, 1994. pp. 197-227.

Duberman, Martin. *Paul Robeson*. New York: Knopf, 1988.

Ellison, Ralph. *The Invisible Man*. New York: New American Library, 1952.

Finkelman, Paul, ed. *Race, Law, and American History: The African-American Experience*. New York: Garland Press, 1992.

Franklin John Hope. *From Slavery to Freedom: A History of African Americans*. New York: McGraw-Hill, 1994.

Gates, Henry L. "Black demagogues and pseudo-scholars." The New York Times. July 20, 1992.

Golden, Marita and Susan Richards Shreve, eds. *Skin Deep: Black Women & White Women Write About Race*. New York: Nan A. Talese, 1995.

Greenberg, Jack. *Crusaders in the Courts: How a Dedicated Band of Lawyers Fought For the Civil Rights Revolution*. New York: Basic Books, 1994.

Grier, William H. and Price M. Cobbs. *Black Rage*. New York: Bantam Books, 1969.

Guinier, Lani. The tyranny of the majority: fundamental fairness in representative democracy. New York: Free Press, 1994.

Hacker, Andrew. *Two Nations Black and White, Separate, Hostile, Unequal*. New York: Scribner's, 1992.

Hersey, John. *The Algiers Motel Incident*. New York: Knopf, 1968.

Johnson, Charles. *Middle Passage*. New York: Antheneum, 1990.

Jones, James H. *Bad Blood: The Tuskegee Syphillis Eexperiment*. New York: Free Press, 1993.

Kaufman, Jonathan. *Broken Alliance: The Turbulent Times Between Blacks and Jews in America*. New York: Scribner's, 1988.

Kochman, T. Black and White syles in conflict. Chicago: University of Chicago Press, 1981.

Landsberg, Lynne F. and David Saperstein. *Common Road To Justice: A Programming Manual for Blacks and Jews*. Marjorie Kovler Institute for Black-Jewish Relations of the Religious Action Center of Reform Judaism, 1991.

Lerner, M and C. West. *Jews and Blacks: Let the Healing Begin*. New York: Putnam, 1995.

Lester, J, et al. "Blacks & Jews: The Politics of Resentment." *Reform Judaism*. Fall 94. p.10-19.

Levi, Primo. *If Not Now When?* New York: Summit Books, 1985.

Massey, Douglas S. *American Apartheid: Segregation and the Making of the Underclass*. Cambridge MA: Harvard University Press, 1993.

McIntosh, Peggy. "White Privilege: Unpacking the Invisible Knapsack." Peace and Freedom. July/August 1989

McMilan, Neil R. *Dark Journey: Black Mississippians in the Age of Jim Crow.* Urbana IL: University of Illinois, 1989.

Oliver, Melvin L. and Shapiro, Tom. *Black Wealth/White Wealth: A New Perspective on Racial Inequality.* Routledge, 1995.

Power, F. Clark and Daniel K. Lapsey, eds. *The Challenge of Pluralism: Education, Politics, and Values.* Notre Dame IN: University of Notre Dame, 1992.

Sacher, Howard. *A History of Jews in America.* New York: Knopf, 1992.

Salzman, Jack, ed. *Bridges and Boundaries: African Americans and American Jews.* New York: George Brazillier, 1992

Spiegelman, Art. *Maus: A Survivor's Tale.* New York: Pantheon Books, 1986.

Staples, Brent. *Parallel Time: Growing Up in Black and White.* New York: Pantheon Books, 1994.

Steele Shelby, The Content of Our Character: A New Vision of Race in America. New York: St. Martin's Press, 1990.

Steptoe, Lamont. *Dusty Road: A Vietnam Suite.* Camden NJ: Whirlwind Press, 1995.

Tatum, Beverly Daniel. *Assimilation Blues: Black Familes in a White Community.* New York: Greenwood Press, 1987.

Walzer, Michael. *What It Means to be An American.* New York: Marsilio, 1992.

West, Cornell. *Race Matters.* New York: Vintage, 1994.

_____. *Keeping Faith: Philosophy and Race in America.* New York: Routledge, 1993.

Woodward, C. Vann. *The Strange Career of Jim Crow.* New York: Oxford University Press, 1982.

Wright, Richard. *Native Son.* New York: Harper & Brothers, 1940.

X, Malcolm. *The Autobiography of Malcolm X.* New York: Ballantine Books, 1964.

Acknowledgements

First I would like to acknowledge and thank all of the people interviewed for the book and exhibit who took the time to share with me their stories, thoughts and hopes concerning Jews and Blacks.

From the outset of this project two people have worked very closely to ensure its quality and artistic merit, and to both of them I am deeply indebted. They are: Barbara Torode whose design for the exhibit and book have helped to enhance the visual impact of the work; and Todd Swimmer, who has worked many diligent hours in the darkroom to print the hundreds of proofs needed in preparing the finished prints for both the exhibit and book.

Cheryl Cutrona, Jim Smart, Stacia Friedman, Ayse Gürsan-Salzmann, Stephen Perloff, Andrew Cassel all provided thoughtful editing and proofing for the book. Jay Treat has organized and set up the Face to Face Home Page. Mordechai Rosenstein has contributed the Hebrew calligraphy. To all of these people who have generously and graciously contributed to make this project a success I say thank you. See study-guide section for further acknowledgements.

Financial support for this project has come from:

The Rex Foundation, The Philadelphia Foundation, Peter Kovler Foundation, Memorial Foundation for Jewish Culture, David & Catherine Steinmann, The Frank Strick Foundation, Inc., The Marjorie Kovler Institute for Black-Jewish Relations, Barbara Streisland Program for Black-Jewish Cooperation, Religious Action Center of Reform Judaism, Joel & Nancy Hirschtritt and Richard Master of MCS Industries, Inc.

About the Photographer/Author:

photograph by Archer Ingersoll

Laurence Salzmann, born and raised in Philadelphia, is self-taught as a photographer and film maker. His formal training in anthropology and languages has provided him with the tools to document diverse peoples and cultures.

Salzmann's films and books are widely known and include: films "Eddie," "Alfred," "Song of Rădăuţi, " "Turkey's Sephardim: 500 Years," and "Who's Havin' Fun?," and books: *The Last Jews of Rădăuţi, La Baie/bath scenes and Anyos Munchos i Buenos.* His work has appeared in New York Times Magazine, GEO Magazine and Sabah Newspaper. Over the past twenty years, there have been over fifty exhibitions of his work. He has also documented Mexican village life, Jerusalem's people, shepherds of Transylvania, and residents of Single Room Occupancy Hotels in New York City.

He lives in an inner-city neighborhood of Philadelphia with his wife and daughter, and two always hungry cats.